RELEASE THE PEACE

Tommye Lee Ray

aka
TLR The Midnight Poet

Tommye Lee Ray
Nov-14-2016

Copyright © 2015 by Tommye Lee Ray
Los Angeles, California
All rights reserved
Printed and Bound in the United States of America

Professional Publishing House
1425 W. Manchester Ave. Ste B
Los Angeles, California 90047
323-750-3592
Email: professionalpublishinghouse@yahoo.com
www.Professionalpublishinghouse.com

Cover design: Stevie Rutherford aka Ruth
First Printing: April. 2015
10 9 8 7 6 5 4 3 2 1
ISBN: 978-0-9861557-2-7

No part of this book may be reproduced, stored in a retrieval system or transmitted in any form or by any means without the prior written permission of the publisher—except by a reviewer who may quote brief passages in a review to be printed in a newspaper, magazine or journal.

For inquiries contact: Tommyeleeray@gmail.com

DEDICATION

Without love, care, dedication, vision and encouragement, I would not have been able to begin or continue my life as a writer.

I dedicate this book to…

My Mother Lonene
Grand Ma-Fannie my beloved grandmother
My Empress (wife)
Daisaku Ikeda my life mentor
Joseph Thomas
Stevie Rutherford my writing coach

TABLE OF CONTENTS

Preface VII
My Vow 13
King of Peace 15
No Justice (Justice?) 16
Step Into Your Feelings 17
Love is a Gift 20
Tribute to Lady D 21
Release the Peace 23
Free to Fly 24
I Am the Beginning 25
Black-Centennial Salute '76 27
Magnolia 30
Peace Officer 31
Voice of Justice 33
Life Traveler 35
Man-Fathers 37
Light 39
Life 40
Essence Pure 41
Continue 42
Today 43
We Are the Alpha 44
Human Revolution 45
Captain of the Middle Way 46
The Truth of You 47
Again 49
End…Beginning 50
Within 51
Spiritual Heights 52
Africa the Universe 53
Blue Moon Magic 54

Unidad en Diferencia / Unity in Difference	55
Our America Reborn	56
Craig	58
Elegant Determination	59
Connections Beyond	63
A Birthday Wish	64
Shadows in Cloud	65
Natural	67
Quest	68
Cancerous Thorn America!	
Police - Unarmed Black Men Killed!	70
Rare Spirit	73
Winter's Love	75
Enlightened World	77
About the Author	79

PREFACE

I was born in the spring in a little town called Midnight Mississippi. To the unfamiliar Midnight is an <u>unincorporated community</u> in the heart of the Southern Delta Located in <u>Humphreys County</u>, Midnight is north of <u>Louise</u> and southwest of <u>Silver City</u>.

When I was a young boy about seven or eight years old, I was given; what I thought, was a bible verse to recite at Easter Sunday morning service. I still remember it today, 68 years later.

For many years, I discovered what I thought was a bible verse was actually a stanza from a poem by Christina Rossetti, "In the Bleak Midwinter." The poem originally written as a Christmas poem and later in 1906 was put to song and became a Christmas carol by Gustav Holst.

The verse (poem) had a profound effect on me. After the recital, and for the very first time, I began writing my own poetry. However, at the time I did not consider it poetry. I called my writings "Thoughts for Grand Ma-Fannie."

Between the years of seven and ten years old, I spent most of my school breaks staying with my grandparents. Ma-Fannie suffered severely from arthritis for as long as I remember. She was such a great spirit; always giving to help others in any way she could. I would watch as she moved about in great pain not letting anything stop her.

Despite her disability, she had a beautiful flower garden and would spend hours tilling the soil; tending her flowers; one of her most favorite things to do. She tended her garden at every opportunity

I saw how much she really liked her flowers. I think it was a way for me to connect to something she loved so dearly, I starting going to her garden and writing about her flowers.

When we would sit together, admiring the day, I would read my thoughts to her about her beautiful flower garden. Ma-Fannie would pat me on my head, and just cry tears of joy and tell me, how well I wrote, and how much she loved my words. Later when I was about ten years old I became a paperboy for the rural, *Grit Newspaper*. The newspaper offered a poetry writing contest. I decided to submit one of my writings about Ma-Fannie's flowers. Much to my surprise I won my first contest and five dollars; and oh my, the praise Ma-Fannie heaped upon me!

When I was twelve years old, my beloved Ma-Fannie passed away. I felt an enormous loss and a great shock to my soul. I stopped writing poetry. Many years passed without me penning a single word.

Fate has a way of changing our lives. At 18 years old, I was sent into the Vietnam War. It was there I found my voice again. I have continued my love affair with poetry, despite being wounded in the War, I tour the US in my one man presentation celebrating the life of Dr. Martin Luther King Jr. Surviving cancer, a heart attack and life's challenges; I continue the joys of writing.

RELEASE
THE
PEACE

My Vow

I awaken with the morning sunrise
Bowing before the rising sun
The seat of enlightenment
I close my eyes and gaze out upon
This Earth filled with
Misery and violence
A bottomless sea of negativity
Opening my eyes
To my universe within
Looking beyond the chaos
Evoking the Universal Law of
Love – Nam-myoho-renge-kyo

Rising from my seat of enlightenment
I step boldly into my every day world
With the spirit of humanity
I move forward
With each of you my
 Brothers my sisters of
Planet Earth
Carrying out The Vow
And through our action
As a human being
The world's winters always
Turn into springs
We are one with each other
In life to absolutely
Continue moving forward
Toward the next hundred years
With deep determination

Fostering youthful spirits
And world is peace being is achieved
Through connections one to one
Moment by moment
 by moment…

King of Peace

Dr. King a man of soul
A man of love
Forever in heart
A Prayer a prayer for the
All Mighty God
A believer of righteousness
Crusader for peace
In his heart love and harmony
For people of every continent
Though sometimes hurt
To the path of forgiveness
His mind always remained
He is now gone
Yet his memory will live on
The world will forever speak
Of a man with a heart
So mild and meek
A man who gave his life
For yours and mine
The sake of all human kind
The unity and love that was bestowed
Throughout this land shall never be forgotten
We will always remember him
Not just a man of color but of all humanity
His life now rest in heavenly domain
His deeds for the sake of humanity
Will forever reign?

No Justice (Justice?)

Walking home between raindrops
Trayvon - innocent – silent night
life splashed strawberry red
on green grass, justice is where?

Step Into Your Feelings

In this Saha world
Where people are used, abused, confused
To be controlled, don't do this don't do that
 Digging into your soul
Trying to destroy your dreams
Telling you to step into reality
No! No! No!
Step out of their reality
Step into your feelings
The reality - the real reality – is
We are already worthy
There is no test to pass
Said there is no test to pass
And sin – sin is just a
Man made abomination
To foster control by others

Step out of their reality
Step out of their reality
Step into your feelings
Into your feelings

The reality is we are already worth
We have come here to thrive and prosper
To live this grand human experience
In light hearted joy
Not *just* struggle in pain
We have come here to have fun
As we learn and grow
We have come to harvest our desires

With the absolute knowledge that
We can have it all – We can have it all
Once we learn how to handle our energies
Meaning our emotions, our feelings

We have come here with
A guaranteed freedom of choice
Mandated by the very
Mandated by the very
Nature of our existence
The time has come for us
To polish our diamonds inside!
The time has come for us
To exercise our birthright
We are caught in no one's web!
We are bound by no circumstances!
We are victim of no one's conditions!
We are beings who possess the sacred ability
To implant any outlandish desires
Out limitless minds can conceive

We possess unregulated, unrestricted uncontested
Freedom of choice no matter what those choices

Step out of their reality
Step into our feelings

It is time to wake up, it time we remembered
How we made those choices happen
It's time to take our heads out of the sand
It's time to accept that what we get in this life
It ain't no accident

Step out of their reality
Step out of their reality

Step into our feelings

It's time for us to stop creating
From improper default settings
We must began to remember
How to make those choices happen
Remembering the secrets of
The ancient wisdom we once knew
So well before recorded history
Wisdom that allowed us to
Create our passion with simple intent

You deserve it all!
You deserve it all!
Your aspiration realized!
No matter what they may be
You have only to want it and
Feeel it! Feeel it!
And a whole life of
Extraordinary happiness yours
Said extraordinary happiness is yours
Not can be, will be
This a cosmic guarantee
Step Into Your Feelings

Love is a Gift

To experience the greatest love
It is not necessary to receive in
Return
Benefits are automatic
Though the mind
May perceive such as
Truth

Receiving love only serves
To activate that which has
Always laid dormant within

The greatest love one can
Experience is that which
Awaken with another being
The feeling or love without
Expectations

A Tribute to Lady Di

I cried for Lady Di
I cried for Lady Di
I cried for Lady Di today
why?

We were miles and worlds apart
I was born a sharecroppers son
down in Midnight, Mississippi
she on the European continent
to status and wealth

Her European ancestors
colonized my African ancestors
Yes, I cried for Lady Di
why?

Because she had hands that
stretched across time and space
beyond the boundaries of
race, religion, and class
Her hands touched the
children of the world
From the starving children in Bosnia
AIDS victims of India
to the children of the mine fields in
Angola, Africa and more

Though challenged
year after year
she never relented

constantly giving of her life
for the sake of
humanity
She is a Universal Queen
a child of the Universe
a queen with great jewels
and treasures of the
heart.

So frail yet so strong
a gentle quick smile
eyes sparkling, glowing like
a windblown candle in the dark.

She is the gold of the Universe
her spirit forever flowing
through the wind
and dancing with the
night
Lady Di I love your
Life

Release the Peace

Release the peace!
Release the peace!
Release the peace!
Passion from within
People are the ones
Passion from without
Positive people shout out
Peace!
Enriching our soul
Empathy making us whole
Energizing our spirit, existence is gold
Peace!
Cultivating courage, confidence and consciousness
Capabilities, cooperation, connecting us as one
Cosmic energy activated from within
Creating peace in the community
Today we begin
Peace
Energizing!
Elevating!
Educating!
Everyone!
Everywhere!
Peace!

Free to Fly

A gentle free breeze
placid, spiritual, powerful
so powerful
yet
Touching me so gentle
like a thousand woodwinds
vibrating in my soul
ascending my life to
new heights

Gentle free breeze
gentle free breeze

I AM the Beginning

Why can't I know my name?
It was taken from me years ago
Washed into the ocean
Along with the blood and tears of my ancestors
As with the dead, it never made to the far away land.

Zingha, Fatima, Amadi, Jahi
are now Fannie, Jim, Toby, Tom
My name is gone
there's nothing I can do
It was taken away from me years ago
Washed into the ocean.

But , who I am is here
and can never go away
I am the beginning
After the IAM, who is the beginning I am
I am poetry in my heart is the beauty
of the first words to be written
Given to me from
The I AM

I am Art
What I see and what I am
is transformed into what is seen
created with the soul
Given to me from
The I AM

I am Music
What I hear and what I am
is heard and experienced
The sound of the soul
All given to me from
The I AM

I can't know my name
but I do know who I am
I am the Beginning
After the
I AM

Black-Centennial Salute '76

As the freedom train cranks it's engines
and prepares for it's journey across
America
Bringing cheers and greetings
to this nation's beginning
We know in actuality it is thirteen
calendar years too early
but
From a moralistic point of view it is

 200 years too late America

As my eyes focus on the conductor of the train
my mind travels back to 1777
 I see
Ole George Washington
Astride his silver grey stallion
   riding off to war
I can imagine ole george saying
  'tis a great thing I do today Martha

For the freedom of our nation is at hand
  and I must wield my sword
For the absolute freedom of America

He may also say to his hundred or more slaves
Now you boys and girls mind
Martha while I am gone or
I shall reward you with the hell of a whip's lashes
  then sell your black asses for a barrel of molasses.

Them there is Thomas Jefferson
An elegant and scholarly gentleman
   speaking six languages
No doubt knowing how to say the word
   --igger in each one!

Elegant humanity lost to his
Purposing laws severely restricting
Free Blacks entrance to
The state of Virginia

It's 200 years too late America!

As the freedom train continues on its way
I see guards standing at its doors
I am reminded of George Wallace
   standing in the school doors of an Alabama
Shouting!

Segregation Forever! Segregation Forever!

The clanking of the trains wheels against the steel rails
   brings to my mind the thought of
Thousands of Brothers and Sisters
Unjustly imprisoned behind
   clanking jail doors

Listening to the squealing sound of the train's whistle
   sickens my soul
With the remembrance of how painful and sorrowful
   the sound must have been as Emmett Till screamed!
 While being castrated by southern white racists
     down in Mississippi

It's 200 years too late America

There can be on celebration of
America's birthday for me
Not until the senseless killing of my people are stopped!
Not until the ugly dragon's head of
Racism and Oppression
Has been thwarted from America's very soul!

My thoughts could continue forever with citations of
Suffering and ruthlessness America
Has heaped upon Black America
 but

For now the freedom has continued on it's way
  and there is nothing left of its visit 'cept
 The cold steel tracks on which came
And my heart soul and mind are the same to the salute of

AMERICA'S BICENTENIAL
Yes
America, it is 200 years too late!

HAPPY BIRTHDAY America!

Magnolia

Skyscrapers neo light flashing
A tall magnolia tree smiling loudly
Do you need the noise?

A Peace Officer

I met a Peace Officer today
Some say police officer
Yet I say you are a Peace Officer
You had a dream of becoming
This officer at the
Young age of nineteen
Life's travel took you
Into other expressions
On your journey
But today now your dream
Is being realized
Your years and maturity
Family and children
Has brought you full circle
To become this Peace Officer
With a smile bright as the
September Sun
You are that Sun

If commitment to community
Is a deep blue sea
Then you are that Sea
If fairness is a wondrous
Starry night sky
Then you are that Night Sky
Could all these descriptions
Express the soul of
You the police officer
　perhaps…

Though my encounter
With you was brief
I know you to be
A Peace Officer

Voice for Justice

Injustice has become
Like a demon etching itself
Into our souls
Leaving us weak and feeble
Staring to the heavens
Wondering why and how?

Be the voice of justice!

Even if 100 years should pass
It can never be only a
Quietness in the night
The Universe's cosmic rhythm
Shouting back enabling
Justice to be done
If only we continue
To raise our voices
The dawn will come
Winter always turns to spring
Even if at first we are alone
Our voices shouting for
Justice becomes a wave length
Then one, two, three
Catch the rhythm and other will follow
Be that one voice for justice!
If only we continue…
Someone will hear…
Someone will listen…
Someone will…

The treasure tower of our
Life within like a
Tuning fork will begin
Ringing out with compassion
Into the dark of midnight
If only we continue
To be that one voice
For justice in the dark
of midnight.
Without fail the Universal Law of
Love will shine on like a

Thousand points of light
It will shine on, shine on
To not just overcome
But come together
And the dream is now a reality

Life Traveler

Your joyful life condition
Your warm springtime smile
Always **brightening others gloom**
It is there always there

You travel on for world peace
Your mission is the Universe
Knowing the road to freedom
lies within

You touch the depths
of my life beyond the intellect
Where friends are friends in life's
Limitless beginnings.

Your life walking with
the grace of the wind
flowing like the rivers of
time

This physical existence now
departed
the dawn of
new beginning

Throughout this life
your faith remained strong
through the last minute
experiencing great joy and
absolute happiness

The joy and happiness
will be more magnificent
the next life - the next life
and
Throughout eternity.

Man-Fathers

Man-Fathers are
short, tall, thin
All colors our
Great Earth can express
You Man-Father are beyond
Just being a male

A Man-Father is to be
Pillars of our Earth
Shoulders for our
Families to stand firm
Upon

Man-Fathers are
Short
Tall
Thin
All colors the
Great Earth can express
You Man-Father are beyond
Just being male

To be a
Man-Father your strength is
A balance the world depend upon

Being a Man-Father is worth
The challenge
Your spirit and love
Have no limit

Stand Man-Father
The world's families need
The strength of your
Shoulders

Light

Like the lotus flower
growing in a deep
muddy swamp
Its petals are rich
And more fragrant
Because of the deep
Struggles it has endured
Opening the light of
Joy with each heart encountered
Your life, so rich so, powerful
So filled with compassion
A thousand points of
Light is reflected
Through your
Hope

Life

In the distance your smile
Showing through the
Beauty of your eyes
like joyful rays of
morning sunrise
Tho' dark clouds hovering
in the skies
yet
Unable to shadow the
Blissfulness of
Life
within

Essence Pure

Your Spirit dances
In the moonlight
Pure
Your life is the
Universe itself

Continue

Assailing the highs…
The lows…
Deep within you
The search of life's
Un-ending quest to
be free
Consent storms rage
Again, again
again…
still
You continue to grow
In life
For if it is to be so
You must continue

Today

Success is our goal
Tomorrow
Is our mission
Yester
Is our legacy we leave behind
For a new generation
Each
Moment is our challenge
Let's take the chance
Together we journey
Life is good
Live it well

We are the Alfa
The Omega

Spiriting forth from
Mother Earth's Africa
Us All
We travel the universe
Life time after life time
Take this hand
My brother, my sister
We will live, love and
Build a nation of hope
to the future
with the genius of our
Spirits

Human Revolution

Many obstacles falling
Into your path
Many tears shed
The pain sometimes unbearable
But the tears, the pain
The endless battles has made
Your life greater
They are the source of
The joys, the happiness
Like the tall, powerful
Mighty Oak Tree
Your roots grow and
still deeper into
Life's soil
These challenges release
Your peace within

Captain of the Middle Way

A Captain of responsibility
His one constant thought
The life condition of the shipmates
Still though able to
Steering the rudder in
The face of danger
Even in times of the mate's discontent
A Captain of the Middle Way
Whose action and intent
Is always the
Heart of the people

The Truth of You

The truth is that
Each of us must ultimately
Answer to yourselves
Regarding our choices in life
One that resonates
Deeply within us
Thus, your first loyalty
is to yourself
Living your own life
As authentically as possible
When you are most yourself
Your are a risk taker
A trailblazer forging your own path
Rather than following anyone's lead
Have the courage to
Boldly assert yourself
And allow your own star
Standing alone when necessary
It is crucial to fulfilling your life's purpose
There are many ways
You could choose to express
Your core sense of singleness
This need to be an original pioneer
Your independence, autonomy and freedom
Are important
Being the sole proprietor of self
Within as little external need as possible
They are expressions of

Your inner life
On your own terms
By your own creativity and dictates
Do this you will be happy
And in harmony with you

Again

Assailing the highs
The lows…
Deep within you
The search of life's
Un-ending quest to be free
Consent storms rage
Again, again
again…
still
You continue to grow
In life
For if it is to be so
You must continue

End....Beginning

The end can be
A wonderful beginning
The beginnings of
Morning's dawn
The eve of dusk
The beauty of each can
be seen with the
soul's eye
For in reality the
Dawn or dusk never
ends or begins
they continue…
So let's be
The experience
We share

Within

In the distance your smile
Showing through the
Beauty of your eyes
Like joyful rays of
morning sunrise
Tho' dark clouds hovering
in the skies
yet
Unable to shadow the
Blissfulness of
Life deep
Within

Spiritual Heights

Placid, spiritual, powerful
Your faith moves my
Life to
New Heights

Africa the Universe

When your skyscrapers reached into the heavens
And your rockets reached the moon
And points beyond
Our vision expanded together to manifest
Great dreams and fly and sour into the
 Vaulting heights of human imagination
We knew what could be then
We know what can be now
From Nubia, Egypt, Ghana, Mali to the Songhai
From Russia to China, Japan, Venezuela
To the Czech Republic, Canada,
The United States and Mexico
Through the depth and breadth of this blue Earth
Great cultures and wondrous civilizations
Which bear the stamp of our original Humanity
We have through our Ancestors
Stood as ancient precursors
To all things both storied and unsung
That we have done
And we claim our unity
Together for all times
Now among the vastness of this blue Earth
 Stages of human civilizations
Many brilliant examples emerge
From whence did we come?
We sprang forth from the universe itself
Setting our bare feet down into fertile soil
Of mother Africa from where the
World itself is born
 Mother Africa!

Blue Moon Magic

When I was diagnosed
With stomach cancer
I complained from
So much pain
Never once did you say
Be quiet and listen
No you simply replied
That is why I am here baby
Just relax and let me
I will be with you
As long as time takes
How I love this spirit
So beautiful as yours
Bringing joy to my soul
You are my Magic
For an eternity
You come once in
A Blue Moon
Stay my Magic
Stay My Magic

Unidid En Diferencin / Unity in Difference

Em este gram pccamp de genta
No bemos buscar las differencias
Al contrato debriamos esplorar
Nuestra similaridades

Las diferencias se manifestan
pur su propin cuenta
es facil verlas

Para enterder la existencia
De esta invisible telarana
Que nos une en harmonia

Debmos experimatar, abazar, prender
y sentie la Algeria que esta diferencias
ses esprean en nuestra vidas

Entones y solo sntones
sentriemos las profundidad
de ley universal
Nam-myoho-renge-kyo
Que nose ne en hermosa harmonia

In this vast ocean of people
Seek not the differences
On the contrary we should explore
the similarities

The difference manifest
on their own
it is easy to see them

To understand the existence
of this invisible web
that unites us

We must experience, embrace, learn
and feel the happiness these
differences express in our lives

Then and only then
will we experience the profundity
in which this Universal Law
Nam-myoho-renge-kyo
Unites us in beautiful harmony

Our America Reborn

We are now a new America
Reborn of a new -
American Human Revolution
A bloodless revolution
No guns no bombs
Youthful lives no longer lost
A new American Human Revolution
-Within the soul the mind the spirit.
America is again the promise of humanity
The bastion of freedom
Our time for change has come
Let us be the change
We wish to see
A time has come for holding hand
Red hands, Black hands
Brown hands, yellow hand, white hands
Children, mothers, fathers
Joining hands from Jamestown
To the Bronx - Appalachia
To the church steps in
Birmingham Alabama - from the
Cotton fields of Midnight, Mississippi
To the streets of Memphis, Tennessee
Hand in hand a family called America
Our time has come for America to
Ascend the mountain top
The mountain top of inclusion
For all that America is...
A new American Human Revolution

Will bring about a change in the
Individual, changing the nation
Changing the world
Cleansing soul, mind and spirit
And once again together
We lift every voice and sing
America, America the beautiful
With amber waves sea to shining sea
From the beaches of Hawaii to the
Banks of the Nile River

Joining hands around the globe
America a lighthouse of humanity for

A world that stands as one
Under our colors waving
Red, white and blue
We the people, together stand
Our hope indivisible with
This new wind of change
Wrapped arm in arm around
Our new -
America Reborn

Craig

Joy to this world
  This great man Craig is born
Most memorable to me is
      Your huge hardy laugh
          And that great smile
             I never saw you without

That laugh, that smile
      It was comforting to so many
I remember how you
  Could make one laugh
      Even on their lowest ebb

Joy to this world
 This great man Craig is born
      Always you were true
         To the life you lived
You brought joy to this world
     And to all whom you encountered

With us your smile, that joy
    Will remain always
    Ever and ever
Always…

    This great man

Elegant Determination

Gliding as she moves
like a small humming bird
floating in mid air
Her small brush sometimes
trailing behind in hand
reminding me of the
Spanish ballerina dancer
Angela Oliver
When she walks every step
is elegance with precision
yet so unpretentious
simply natural she is
Her hands fitting into
plastic latex
with the delicacy of a
skill surgeon
into surgical gloves
I marvel as she talks with

her hands

fingers moving with such

rhythms

Across the great expanse

of the floor

her mop flows

reminding me of

brush strokes by

Leonardo di ser Piero da Vinci

painting the Mona Lisa

What pleasure my

soul receives

Experiencing her mission

carried through with

such dedicated joy

and poetic spirit

Alas!

I know not her origin

my sense says

Latin decent

hence her reminder

of Angela

Her name I know not

yet as I marvel from afar

she reminds me of

Rosa Parks quiet spirit

bringing within me these

thoughts

Hence forth whatever the task

given me of my work

worthy or not it is

I will make myself worthy

of the task

I shall endeavor to

complete it with

as much

Style

Determination

Elegant

and

Grace

Tommye Lee Ray ❦ 62

As does the unknown

cleaning lady in the

tall building across the way

my apartment

Connections Beyond

My Spirit so deeply
Connected to your soul
No matter who is in your heart
Whoever may enters your heart
My space is forever in its place
Whoever shall enter my heart
Never can they claim the place reserved
Especially for your heart
We are like the wind and the rain
When they blow and flow at once
They cannot be found
If I traveled beyond each galaxy
Still the depths of emotions
If I took every drop of
Water from the Red Sea
Distinguished one by one
Each grain of sand
From the Sahara Desert other
Pebble by pebble
The emotions cannot
Measure the depths of
Emotions in my soul
They are both simply there together

A Birthday Wish

May your birthday footie's
  be filled to the brim with
Lots of good health
Lots of food friends
Lots of satisfying work
Lots of well wishes
If you don't get any of this stuff
Just take the
Stocking with the sewed up toe
  and be ok with that
Million dollars that came inside

Shadows in Clouds

His Demons rise with him
Morning after morning
With inexhaustible energy
Tearing after the fiber
of his innermost soul
Like cheese he is shredded
until

A frail pale frame
Swaying wearily against the
Brilliant September noon sun
With graying scraggly beard
Frazzled shoulder length hair
    Swaying gently, wearily
      waiting...
         waiting...
Endless morning and
   the mornings still lingers
  in his mouth with taste of
Yesterday's Ripple Wine
  swaying, gently wearily
    swaying
Reaching, plucking the leaf from a
  low, low swinging branch
Lifting upwards and
   letting fly the leaf
    sailing, drifting lazily down
   upon

September noon winds
  remembering the yesteryears
    gone fast

He smiles quietly with
  a sudden sparkle in his eyes
    remembering joys of
      yesteryears…
Before demons came

When he like the leaf
was green, free, sailing…
    and he smiles
      remembering…
Mozart, Schubert, Kant
Schreiner, Billie Jean
  and he smiles…

Natural

A queen
yet
simple beauty is
hers to command
Poise, grace, unsurpassed
Many who assume to hold the
Truths of her jewels and treasures
untold
Her quietness engulfs you
like the breath of a
still night

Leaving a calmness of
a moonlight white
sandy beach in paradise
Natural beauty enshrined in the
hour glass of time to be
marveled - pleasured

Quest

Deep dark, rich
Liquid pools glisten
  with a soft touch
    of silver moonlight
Her eyes
Reveal the soul of
Her life in search of

She has traveled timeless
roads in search of truth

Many marveled in Her
physical beauty
Taking more than giving
still
Her eyes sparkle with
Hope of the Vision
Seen only by Her though
quite real

None see or hear
Though She is aware of
possessed beauty

Still more wanting of understanding
More is taken of Her
She gives more
  Yet
She falters not in the quest of
Her search
The Vision is clear

The revel in Her beauty
is un-concerning to Her

The sparkle of Her eyes
A quick gentle smile acknowledge
and
Travels on in search of the
True Vision within
That must and will be realized
    innermost

NO one knows
    Yet everyone will…

Cancerous Thorn America!
Police - Unarmed Black Men Killed!

I am a **Thorn** when oppressed!
  I am a gentle spirit…

Hands Up Don't Shoot!

In the past decade alone these
Unarmed Black Men killed
Michael Brown – Ferguson, Missouri
I am a **Thorn** when oppressed!
  I am a gentle spirit…
Timothy Stanberry – Brooklyn, New York
You America have made me
  into this **Thorn**
into this thorn
A **Thorn** punctures when
  stepped upon
Shan Bell – Queens, New York
A **Thorn** lingers and festers
  Causing cancerous harm
I am a **Thorn** when oppressed!
  I am a gentle spirit…
Oskar Gran – Oakland, California
Your soldiers have marched
  into my community, my mind,
my soul, my spirit
I am crushed from the weight
  of their boots
Erin Campbell - Portland, Oregon
But soldier's feet do tire

Rest your feet soldiers
   upon this pleasant
Earthly soil
Alonzo Ashley – Denver, Colorado

Up soldier! Up soldier!
There is no time! There is no time!
We have another one! Another one!
Wendell Adams - New Orleans, Louisiana

White police kill two
Black persons every week
From 2006 to 2012

On with those boots soldier
Hurry! Hurry!
We have another one! Another one!
Jonathan Ferrell – Charlotte, North Carolina
Ouch! Damn **Thorn**!
On with those boots solider
There is no time!
Erick Garner - Staten Island, New York
I am a **Thorn** when oppressed!
   a **Thorn** lingers and festers
Causing cancerous harm
Michael Brown – 2014 – Ferguson, Missouri

1847 Dred Scott sues for his
and his wife's freedom
Supreme Court Chief Justice 1847
Roger Taney speaks a decision

A Black man has no rights
A white man is
bound To respect

No rights a white man
  is bound
I am a **Thorn**
A **Thorn** punctures when oppressed
  and **stepped** upon
Causing cancerous harm
No Rights a white man
  is bound to respect?
I am a **Thorn** when oppressed
  and stepped upon!
   Causing cancerous harm
     Wake up! Wake up!
There is a **Thorn**
 in your foot
America!

A Rare Spirit

Assured like falling leaves
Autumn anticipations
Powered by your faith

I encountered this
Life…
She danced on the river
one day
Tho' youthful in years
Life circumstances compelled
her into distant adulthood
I young unaware of
many things
unable to say words
that rang in my thoughts

Unable to meet her eyes
with mine
to touch her lips
her fingertips
My words, my emotions
held to thoughts only

She danced one day
on the river

Again my thoughts came
I remained silent…

The vibrancy of her movements
The wisdom of her physical

yet…
In her distant eyes
Sparkled the wanting
of
a childhood gone early…

I encountered this
Life…
She danced on the river
one day
She will forever remain
remembered
here in my thoughts

Winter's Love

Crack is a Winter's Love
a misleading spirit
disguising itself with
Metaphors of crisp winter winds
and festive holidays
yet
Lurking in the trenches
are destructive forces
Brining misery to the
soul
Emotions like a face left bare to the
Winter's wind -
Rough, dry, flaking, dull and lifeless
The Crack of the Winter's Love
Bringing dry dispositions
Stealing the natural moister
of the soul
By day and by night
A thief robbing what nature has
So graciously given

Take a moment to remember…
Remember the glow
Before that chilling
Winter's Love came
Those were the times of
Warmer seasons when we
Drank the wine, danced
Ate the fruits

Stop, think remember…

But alas back to the arms of our
Lover we fall
Crack Cocaine is a
Winter's Love

Enlightened World

For thirty odd years
we have with great
Human Revolution
Polished the mirror of our lives
We have become the
Looking glass of each other
Let us now not be afraid that
Our lives without fail
Will open the window within
And The Ninth conscious will reveal
Depths of our - True Cause
Nam-myoho-renge-kyo

About the Author

Tommye Lee Ray lives with his wife who is also his muse, in Los Angeles, California. He is currently working on his fourth book of poetry and his autobiography.

TLR THE MIDNIGHT POET